ENVIRONMENTAL ISSUES

SEA LEVELS AND ICE CAPS

By Emilie Dufresne

KidHaven
PUBLISHING

Published in 2020 by
KidHaven Publishing, an Imprint of Greenhaven Publishing, LLC
353 3rd Avenue
Suite 255
New York, NY 10010

Edited by: Holly Duhig
Designed by: Amy Li

Cataloging-in-Publication Data

Names: Dufresne, Emilie.
Title: Sea levels and ice caps / Emilie Dufresne.
Description: New York : KidHaven Publishing, 2020. | Series: Environmental issues | Includes glossary and index.
Identifiers: ISBN 9781534530683 (pbk.) | ISBN 9781534530386 (library bound) | ISBN 9781534531703 (6 pack) | ISBN 9781534530645 (ebook)
Subjects: LCSH: Sea level--Climatic factors--Juvenile literature. | Ice caps--Juvenile literature. | Global warming--Juvenile literature. | Climatic changes--Juvenile literature.
Classification: LCC GC89.D847 2020 | DDC 551.45'8--dc23

Printed in the United States of America

CPSIA compliance information: Batch #BS19KL: For further information contact Greenhaven Publishing LLC,
New York, New York at 1-844-317-7404.

Please visit our website, www.greenhavenpublishing.com. For a free color catalog of all our high-quality books, call toll free 1-844-317-7404 or fax 1-844-317-7405.

Words that look like **this** can be found in the glossary on page 24.

CONTENTS

ICE CAPS

The polar ice caps are two large areas of ice at each end of the Earth.

THE ARCTIC IS AN AREA THAT CONTAINS A LARGE ICE PACK THAT FLOATS ON THE ARCTIC OCEAN. IT ALSO INCLUDES VERY COLD, ICY PARTS OF GREENLAND, RUSSIA, AND OTHER COUNTRIES.

ANTARCTICA IS A CONTINENT. IT IS COVERED IN THE LARGEST ICE SHEET ON EARTH.

ELEPHANT FOOT GLACIER, GREENLAND

Glaciers, ice caps, and ice sheets are different types of ice. Ice caps and sheets are large areas of ice that have been there for a long time. Glaciers are slow-moving bodies of ice.

SEA LEVELS

The sea level is where the top of the sea comes up to on the land. The sea level can be used to measure how high or low things are, such as mountains and valleys.

WELCOME TO 2020m ABOVE SEA LEVEL

← NZ's HIGHEST CAFÉ

← SKYLINE WALK 1.5-2 HRS RETURN

← BACK TO BASE TRAIL 1HR DESCENT

Measuring the sea levels helps us to know how quickly global warming is making the sea levels rise, and can help us to predict what will happen in the future.

GLOBAL WARMING

Global warming is the rise in the average temperature of the Earth. Global warming is made worse by **greenhouse gases**. These gases trap the heat from the sun, making the Earth warmer – like a greenhouse!

PLANES, CARS, AND FACTORIES ALL MAKE GREENHOUSE GASES BY BURNING FOSSIL FUELS.

Global warming causes many problems, such as changes in weather patterns, loss of plant and animal **habitats**, melting ice caps, and rising sea levels.

MELTING ICE AND RISING SEA

As the Earth is getting warmer, the ice caps are melting more than they usually do. Scientists believe that around two-thirds of the rise in sea levels is due to ice falling into the sea.

The sea levels are also rising because the water is **expanding**. When water gets warmer, the **particles** inside it start to move more. This means that the same amount of water takes up more space when it is warmer.

STUDYING ICE SHEETS

Scientists can dig through layers of ice like **archaeologists** dig through layers of earth. Each layer of ice can tell us a lot about the **climate** at the time it was formed.

A 100,000-YEAR-OLD ICE SAMPLE WAS TAKEN IN ANTARCTICA THAT WAS 1.9 MILES (3 KM) DEEP.

LAYERS OF ICE

Ice samples let us see how different our climate is today compared to hundreds of years ago. They can show us the amount of snowfall at different times, and what levels of different gases were in the air when the ice formed.

LOSS OF HABITATS

Lots of animal and plant habitats are being lost because of melting ice caps. Without the ice, animals such as seals, penguins and polar bears struggle to eat enough food and raise their **young**.

RINGED SEAL

TURTLES USE THE CORAL REEFS TO FIND FOOD.

Rising sea levels mean that the beaches where this hawksbill turtle lays its eggs could soon be underwater. Coral reefs are also affected by rising sea levels.

This Adélie penguin needs sea ice to help it catch krill in the winter. Without the ice, the penguins can't catch food to feed their young and they could soon become **endangered**.

These Laysan albatrosses often build their nests on islands. These islands could easily be swept away by the wind or flooding caused by a rise in sea levels.

STORMS AND FLOODING

Melting ice caps and rising sea levels can make the weather more extreme. Storms on the coast are likely to be more damaging. These storms are also likely to be worse because of global warming.

HEAVY RAINFALL CAN LEAD TO RIVERS BURSTING THEIR BANKS.

Floods are much more likely to occur. Global warming can create more moisture in the air, which means rainfall might be heavier and happen more often.

WORLD UNDERWATER

As the sea levels continue to rise, lots of our land will end up underwater and many people's homes will be lost.

Lots of coastal areas will be affected by the rise in sea level. Miami in the United States, Shanghai in China, and Alexandria in Egypt could all be underwater if the global average temperature rises just 7°F (4°C).

ALEXANDRIA, EGYPT

MIAMI, U.S.

SHANGHAI, CHINA

HOW WE CAN HELP

There are lots of things we can do to slow down the rising sea levels. Here are a few ideas to get you started.

TURN IT OFF

Lights, video game consoles, and chargers all use a lot of energy that produces greenhouse gases. Make sure to turn all plugs and switches off at the wall when you're not using them.

TURN IT DOWN

Heating and cooling down your home uses a lot of fossil fuels. Turn down your heating and air-conditioning. Why not put on, or take off, a sweater instead?

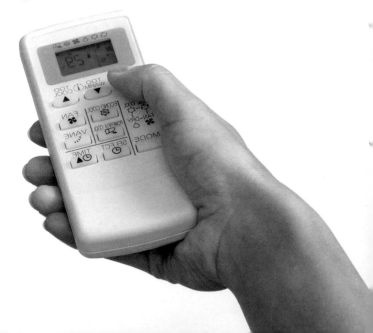

WALK WHEREVER YOU CAN

Whether you're going to school, the park, or the store, walking instead of driving keeps **emissions** from getting into the air.

SPREAD THE WORD

Now that you know how to help slow down the rising sea levels, spread the word. Tell your friends all about what the problems are and how they can help.

GLOSSARY

archaeologists	historians who study buried ruins and ancient objects
climate	the common weather in a certain place
continent	a very large area of land, usually made up of several countries
emissions	the harmful gases produced by cars and other vehicles
endangered	when a species of animal is in danger of going extinct
expanding	becoming larger
fossil fuels	fuels, such as coal, oil, and gas, that formed millions of years ago from the remains of animals and plants
greenhouse gases	gases in the air that trap the sun's heat
habitats	the natural environments in which animals or plants live
particles	extremely small pieces of a substance
young	an animal's offspring or babies

INDEX